Piano • Vocal • Guitar

Title: STARTING OV

By: CHRIS STAPLETON

ISBN 978-1-70513-112-1

Visit Hal Leonard Online at
www.halleonard.com

Contact us:
Hal Leonard
7777 West Bluemound Road
Milwaukee, WI 53213
Email: info@halleonard.com

In Europe, contact:
Hal Leonard Europe Limited
42 Wigmore Street
Marylebone, London, W1U 2RN
Email: info@halleonardeurope.com

In Australia, contact:
Hal Leonard Australia Pty. Ltd.
4 Lentara Court
Cheltenham, Victoria, 3192 Australia
Email: info@halleonard.com.au

Contents

STARTING OVER

Words and Music by CHRIS STAPLETON
and MIKE HENDERSON

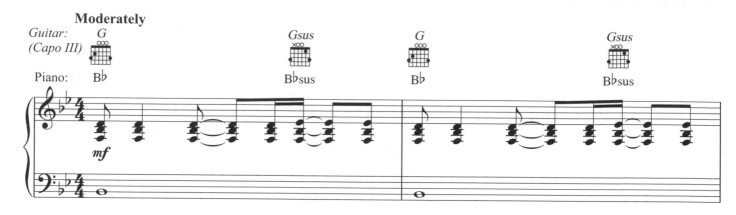

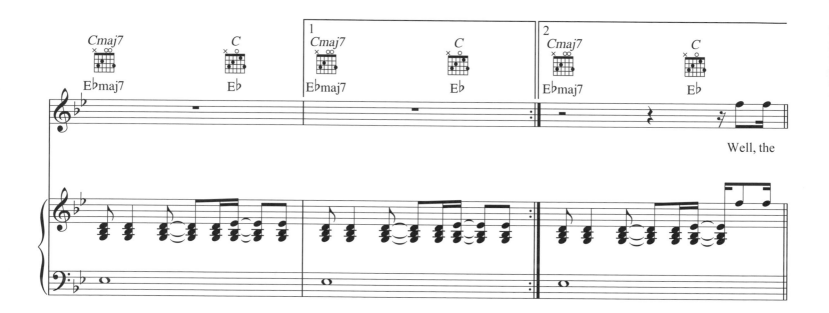

DEVIL ALWAYS MADE ME THINK TWICE

Words and Music by CHRIS STAPLETON
and AL ANDERSON

Moderately fast

* *Guitar tuned to Drop D tuning*

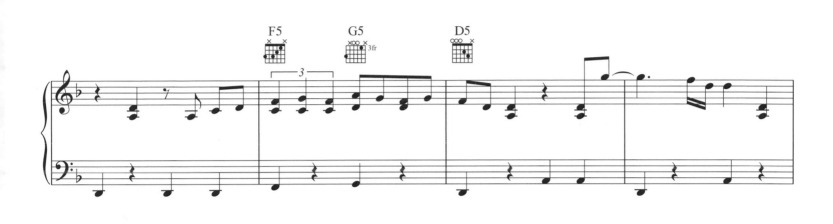

Some

COLD

Words and Music by CHRIS STAPLETON,
DAVE COBB, J.T. CURE
and DEREK MIXON

Slow Rock Ballad

drum groove enters

Girl, the way you broke my heart, it shat-tered like a rock through a
What am I sup-posed to say if an-y-bod-y asks me a-

win-dow. ___
bout you? ___ I guess I'll tell 'em I'm with-out you. ___

JOY OF MY LIFE

Words and Music by
JOHN FOGERTY

WHEN I'M WITH YOU

Words and Music by
CHRIS STAPLETON

Moderate Country Waltz

I'm for-ty years old ___ and it

looks like the end ___ of the rain - bow ain't no ___ pot of gold. ___

The things that I've done ___ I doubt an-y-one ___ will re-mem-ber ___

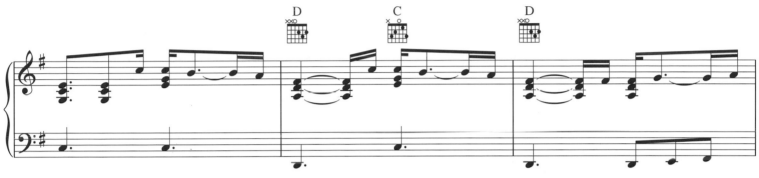

I got a good job ___

and I'm thank - ful to be work - in' ___ when so

ARKANSAS

Words and Music by CHRIS STAPLETON
and MIKE CAMPBELL

Moderate Country Rock, in 2

Took a Nine E - lev - en 'bout a hun - dred and sev - en down a back road, where the white riv - er runs ___ and the south - ern sun ___ makes the kud - zu grow. ___ And what I found ___ in the O - zark moun - tains I ain't

HILLBILLY BLOOD

Words and Music by
CHRIS STAPLETON

Hill - bil - ly blood __ run - nin' through my veins,
Hill - bil - ly blood, __ riv - er runs __ red,
Hill - bil - ly blood, __ thick as ____ the night,

*Guitar tuned to Drop D tuning

MAGGIE'S SONG

Words and Music by
CHRIS STAPLETON

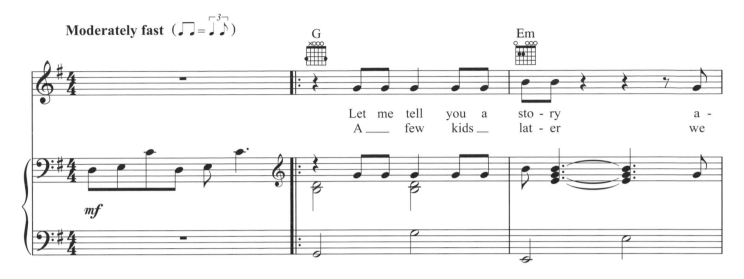

Let me tell you a sto-ry a-
A __ few kids __ lat-er we

bout an old __ friend of mine. Some-bod-y left her in a
moved __ out __ on the farm. And she fol-lowed those __

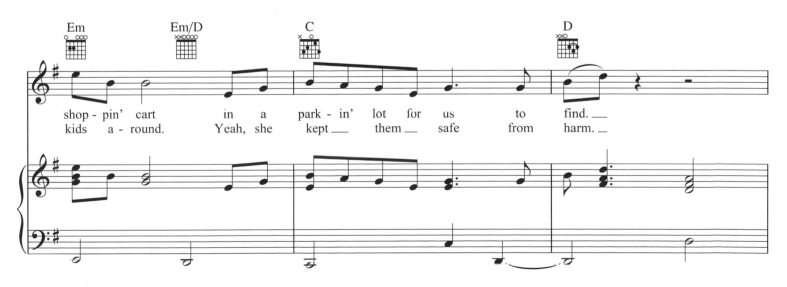

shop-pin' cart in a park-in' lot for us to find. __
kids a-round. Yeah, she kept __ them __ safe from harm. __

WHISKEY SUNRISE

Words and Music by CHRIS STAPLETON
and TIM KREKEL

Guitar tuned to Drop D tuning.

lay __ down to sleep __ and I pray __ I don't o - pen my eyes __

to a whis - key sun - rise. __

Guitar solo ad lib.

The cold __

rit.

OLD FRIENDS

Words and Music by GUY CLARK,
SUSANNA WALLIS CLARK and RICHARD J. DOBSON

WORRY B GONE

Words and Music by GARY NICHOLSON,
GUY CLARK and LEE ROY PARNELL

Moderately

Aw, gim-me just one more puff of that wor-ry be gone.

Guitar solo on D.S.

I'm plann-in' on feel-in' much bet-ter be-fore too long.

I got a

* *Guitar tuned to Drop D tuning*

WATCH YOU BURN

Drop D tuning, down 1 whole step:
(low to high) C - G - C - F - A - D

To the e-vil ones, _____ you know _____ who you are, _____

YOU SHOULD PROBABLY LEAVE

Words and Music by CHRIS STAPLETON,
CHRIS DuBOIS and ASHLEY GORLEY

NASHVILLE, TN

Words and Music by CHRIS STAPLETON
and MORGANE HAYES

you when I had a dream _____ not _____ so long a - go
won't miss me when I'm gone. _____ You're cus - tom - made for mov -

I met _____

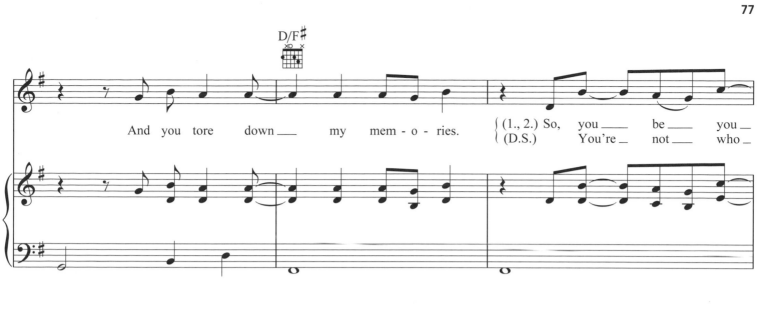

And you tore down ____ my mem-o-ries. { (1., 2.) So, you ____ be ____ you ____
                                            { (D.S.) You're ___ not ___ who ___

____ and I'll ____ be me. ____ }   So long, Nash - ville, Ten - nes - see.
____ you used ____ to be. ____ }

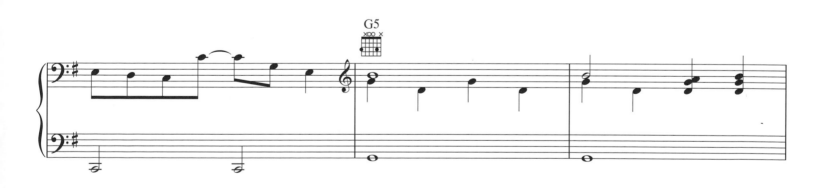

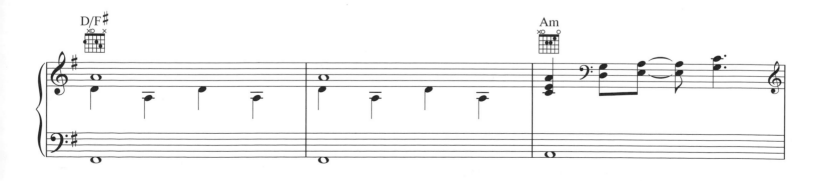

Now you ___   So long, Nash -